OVERFLOW "Trekke

Welcome to the 9th Annual OVERFLOW High School "TREK" Winter Retreat. We are so glad you are here! This weekend is intended to provide space to be with God through rhythms of scripture, prayer, rest, community, time in His creation, and so much more.

This is not just another weekend away for a "mountain top experience", but rather four days of real rest and intentional time with God so that when we get home we can continue following Jesus more deeply and more courageously than before!

Take advantage of this time away from the noise of life to rest and experience intimacy with Jesus. He has been looking forward to this time with you.

With Love,

OVERFLOW Staff

TABLE OF CONTENTS

STUDENT JOURNAL

LEADER GUIDE

THE TREK 2025

RHYTHMS OF RESISTANCE

RHYTHMS OF <u>RESISTANCE</u>

Resistance is a refusal to accept or comply with something or someone. To say "no". To draw a "line in the sand". Scripture speaks to a posture of resistance to anything that opposes God and our flourishing in Him. The world, the flesh and the devil influence away from God and towards idolatry and disobedience. How do we become the kind of people who resist in order to trust Jesus more fully and enjoy freedom in Him.

Ultimately, God does the work to move us towards becoming people of courage and conviction in a culture of compromise. Our part is to obey him and open ourselves to God and His work within us. This weekend we will be engaging in a variety of biblical rhythms and practices of the way of Jesus. These practices are <u>not</u> the end goal but are simply a way for us to turn our attention to God and receive His grace. Any real strength and courage is a gift from God and everything we do is an opportunity to acknowledge, receive and enjoy God's gift of grace and God himself. Let's learn and practice Jesus' rhythms of life together:

<u>PRAYER</u>
Prayer is anything where you're fixing your attention on God, offering yourself to Him and receiving Him. Often prayer is focused time for just that but there are endless ways to pray! We can find strength and peace in Christ as we commune with Him (Philippians 4:4-8). *For more on prayer go to p.49

<u>SCRIPTURE</u>
The Bible, as a whole, communicates one unified true story of God's love for humanity. This story continues with us. Every truth and insight is a gift from God to us. Would you understand and find strength in God's truth as you study, contemplate, and discuss scripture (Hebrews 4:12). For more on reading scripture go to p.53

SILENCE AND SOLITUDE (Quiet & Alone With God)

In our over-busy and hurried society it is vital that we make space in quiet with God. Let's follow Jesus' example of "getting away to quiet places to pray" to receive God's grace through unhurried time with Him (Luke 5:16). For more on silence and solitude go to *p. 54*

FELLOWSHIP IN COMMUNITY

We are not designed to live and follow Jesus alone. God made us for relationships and we need meaningful relationships with other followers of Jesus to encourage and build each other up. Whether it's sharing a meal, surfing or a meaningful conversation, let's develop strong relationships with one another (John 13:34; Acts 2:42-47).

PHYSICAL REST

We were made to work, create, play, but also to REST. Sleep, sit, walk, breath, nap, or whatever is restful for your body. Receive the space to physically rest as means of God's grace and an opportunity to cultivate trust in God's provision (Psalm 23).

GOD'S CREATION

God has created a universe and world full of beauty which points to his power, creativity, and love for all things good and beautiful. Every sunset, ocean breeze, bird chirping, tree swaying, star in the sky is a gift of God's presence and power on display. See it, contemplate it and find strength in it as a reminder of God's grace, creativity, and beauty. (Psalm 19:1; Psalm 8; Psalm 139)

CELEBRATION

Resistance is not the end goal! Joy and freedom is! Whether it's singing worship songs with your community, cheering on a friend, affirming something you appreciate about someone, or moments of silliness and laughter, let's experience joyful celebration together and be strengthened by it! (Philippians 4:4; Psalm 112:1-10)

Guidelines & Expectations

In order to get the most out of our time, it's important we are unified in following the same guidelines and expectations. We will read through each expectation, check the box to indicate you understand and agree. If you aren't comfortable with an expectation, please talk to myself or any OVERFLOW leader so we can get on the same page. Failure to follow these expectations will lead to a conversation and potential consequences as severe as being sent home.

I AGREE TO...

☐ **Be Present:** I understand that the goal of this weekend is to grow in relationship with God and one another. I will do my best to be focused on what is happening in the moment and intentional with my time: a meal, a conversation, a discussion, time with God or whatever it is I am doing.

☐ **Love Others:** I will do my best to treat everyone with dignity, respect and love. I will do my best to not just focus on my own needs and desires but to look to the interest of others. I will be inclusive and inviting. I will resist cliqueness and will pursue meaningful relationships with people outside of my own friend group.

☐ **Be Positive:** I commit to being positive and I will maintain a positive attitude and be flexible. I will not gossip or spread negativity through the group, but will approach an OVERFLOW Leader for guidance and counsel if there is any conflict. I will do my best to have a good attitude about my RV assignment and the OVERFLOW guidelines.

☐ **Be At All Meals:** I will be at all meals as an opportunity to build relationships, to be well-fed, and most importantly, have healthy bowel movements.

☐ **Be At Everything:** I will attend all OVERFLOW meetings, meals, and activities NO MATTER WHAT. I will be on time, at the right location, and have the appropriate attire and materials with me when necessary.

☐ **Be Chivalrous:** [For the Guys] I will be respectful to all ladies. I will open doors, use manners, respect their space and privacy and be mindful of my conversations. I will do everything I can to make the ladies feel loved, respected, empowered and valued.

- [ ] **Receive and Reciprocate:** [For the Ladies] I will receive the respectful and chivalrous acts of the guys with gratitude. I will respect their privacy and be mindful of my conversations. I will do my best to make the guys feel loved, respected, empowered and valued.

- [ ] **No Purple:** I will never be alone or one-on-one with someone of the opposite sex in private. I will not put myself in a situation such that my behavior with anyone could be questioned and will talk to a leader if I need help navigating a particular relationship. I will avoid PDA (ex. holding hands, cuddling, kissing, etc.), which would be a distraction for me and others. I accept adult leaders keeping me accountable.

- [ ] **No Guys in the Girl RV's and Girls in the Guy RV's:** I commit to only be in my RV. Except for designated RV living rooms during free time. I will respect other RVs. I will keep my RV living room clean. I will never be alone with someone of the opposite sex in an RV.

- [ ] **Be Mindful of What I Wear:** Girls | I will cover my Boobs-Butt-Belly-Bra. If I wear leggings, I will cover my bottom with a shirt/sweatshirt. Guys | I will cover up my "man parts" and will only take my shirt off if I'm in or near the ocean.

- [ ] **Staying Safe:** I will stay in sight of the campgrounds and will not go past designated boundaries (we'll go over these once we arrive). I will only go to the beach, ocean, or other free time area if I have told a leader and have someone with me.

- [ ] **Not "Mess Around":** Lets have fun but in the right way! When we say "don't mess around" we mean:
    1. NO Drugs, Alcohol, or Tobacco
    2. NO Firearms, Fireworks or Weapons
    3. NO Electronic Devices
    4. NO Wrestling or Horseplay
    5. NO Altering Physical Appearance Jumping in the RVs, Showering in the RVs, Touching ANY of the buttons in the RVs and Distracting Drivers
    6. NO Leaving campsite by yourself or going to other campsites

- [ ] **Bathroom Etiquette:** I will only use the bathrooms in my RV or the campsite bathrooms. I commit to only poop in the RV bathroom when the campsite bathroom is unavailable. I will knock first. I will clean up after myself. I will only shower in campsite bathrooms.

- ☐ **Respecting the Campground:** I will respect the campground, understanding that other people are here as well. If I see another person, I will greet them kindly.
- ☐ **Nightly RV Affirmations:** Affirm everyone in my RV by the end of the weekend. By the end of this weekend, you will have the privilege of affirming everyone in your RV. This is an important responsibility and something we take very seriously so please do not take this lightly. It is a tremendous gift to give and receive meaningful words of affirmations so give and receive them well. Your RV leaders will let you know who is being affirmed each night.

RV Etiquette:
The RV's have limited waste storage so its important that we agree to:
- ☐ Not use sink in bathrooms and kitchen (running water and waste fills up the tanks quickly)
- ☐ Avoid "#2" unless its an emergency and public bathrooms are in use
- ☐ No showers in RV
- ☐ Follow generator guidelines next to control board

General Guidelines:
- ☐ Don't put it down. . . put it away!
- ☐ Keep all your stuff in your bags (on front or back bed)
- ☐ Always be in pairs (at least)
- ☐ Stay within camp boundaries

Free Time Guidelines:
- ☐ Be inclusive and inviting
- ☐ Be aware of timing
- ☐ Be mindful of other groups
- ☐ Try new things!

Transportation Guidelines:

- ☐ Listen to leaders
- ☐ Respect the driver
- ☐ Throw away all trash IN trash bags
- ☐ Remain seated
- ☐ Do not ask "are we there yet?" or "are we close?"
- ☐ Do not yell or make loud noises

I agree to follow all guidelines and expectations as best I can in order to avoid distractions that may hinder me from growing in my relationship with God and building healthy relationships with others.

X: _____   **Date**: _____
Signature

X: _____
Print Name

Emergency Contact Info

In case of an emergency, all of your leaders will have their cell phones on them. If a leader isn't around, find a pay phone or borrow a phone, if needed. Always call **911** first.

Emergency Contacts:

1. **Emergency Personnel:** 911
2. **Trevor Lawrence:** (714) 328-6391
3. **Sofia Franco** (949) 910-1958

LOCAL HOSPITAL

Goleta Valley Cottage Hospital
Address: 351 S Patterson Ave, Goleta, CA 93111

- □ **Emergency:** 911
- □ **Office Phone:** (805) 967-3411

*In case of an emergency please ask for help and find a phone and call **911***

Optional Activities

There is a ton of free time this weekend. Here are some epic (optional) activities that you should do because you could have FOMO if you don't, but no pressure! Seriously, none! We will provide details each morning about the daily options.

SIGN UPS REQUIRED:

Hike
Let's go on a hike and enjoy God's creation together! A leader will lead this optional activity on Saturday.

OVERFLOW Soft-Top Surfboard Rentals
We have boards for you to use! Use one for an hour and then bring it back so others can try.

OVERFLOW Soft-Top Surf Contest
Join us for our OVERFLOW Soft-Top surf contest judged on quality of wave, execution, creativity, style and overall stoke. Make a team of 4 – all skill levels are welcome!

Co-ed Flag-Football Tournament
Nothing is better than some friendly competition! Make a team of 7-8 (4-5 guys and 3-4 ladies) and meet us on the beach.

Crafts:

- Saturday: Let's watercolor!
- Sunday: We're making bracelets! Join us at the RV Picnic Tables. Make something to remember the trip by.

FRIDAY

THE TREK

Church Time | Debrief

Practices
Which practice from the list
on the introduction pages
most excites you to engage?
Which practice doesn't? How
might God be inviting you to
engage with Him in them?

People
Who is someone you got
  to know better on the ride?

_____

_____

_____

_____

_____

_____

_____

_____

_____

_____

_____

_____

_____

_____

_____

_____

_____

_____

Main Take Away

What is one truth you discovered today?

_____
_____
_____
_____
_____
_____
_____
_____
_____
_____
_____
_____

I Feel...

What is one feeling word to describe where you at right now?
see p. 54

_____
_____
_____
_____
_____
_____
_____

RV Time | *"Where Are You At?"*

It's important for us to learn how to identify themes / seasons in our lives; this helps us see what God is doing and saying. Honesty with God and others is a crucial part of our spiritual formation. This exercise is a way to help us be aware of where we are at with God, share it in the context of a safe group, and offer ourselves to God as we are.

INSTRUCTIONS:
- Browse the pictures and take one that stands out to you. Spend time looking at the picture and reflect on the word written on the back (5 min)
- Read and respond to the questions on next page (5 min)
- One by one, each person will share with the group why they chose that picture and their answer to at least one of the questions. (3-5 min)
- We will each pray for the person to our left after they share. (*p.52 "Intercessory | Praying for Others"*)

GUIDELINES BEFORE YOU BEGIN:
1. **Honor** God, one another and yourself.
2. **Be honest** with what you share but there is no pressure to share anything you don't feel comfortable sharing.
3. **Whatever is shared in the RV stays in the RV**. Anything shared with you is a gift, so treat it as such.
4. **Be a good listener.** Make eye contact when someone is sharing and listen to *understand* ("where they are at?"). This is not a time to give advice or try to "fix" someone or their problems, but rather a time to listen, empathize, and pray.
5. **Ask.** After each person shares we will leave space for 1-2 people to ask follow-up questions related to what they shared. This is an opportunity to be outside of ourselves and be present to another person and show that we listened and we care.

REFLECTION QUESTIONS:

1.   Why did you choose this photo? How does this picture relate to your life in general? How does it connect to where you're at in your relationship with God?

2.   Did the word on the back of the card resonate with you? Is the word something you need or want from God? Does it represent where you're at right now? Maybe it doesn't resonate with you at all! Reflect on that:

3.   How may God be inviting you to *respond* to this?

4.   Is there anything specific you desire, hope for, or need from God right now?

SATURDAY

THE TREK

Saturday | Time with God

PRAYER:

"Father, Son & Spirit - soften my heart, open my eyes, focus my mind, quiet my soul, and strengthen my body. May your Word dwell richly within me."

SCRIPTURE STUDY:

Daniel 1-7

Daniel 1-7 Commentary:

Author: Daniel was a young Israelite noble who was taken captive to Babylon around 605 B.C. He was renamed Belteshazzar by the Babylonian leadership. Daniel lived in Babylon throughout the 70-year captivity of the Jews, and eventually became an administrator over the provincial governors. Daniel was known for having the gift of prophetic dreams and interpretation of those dreams (provided by God Himself!). These gifts gave him influence and favor with Babylonian leadership even though he was a Jew in exile.

Overall Theme: Daniel's prophetic visions offer hope that God will bring all nations under his rule. Daniel's visions are packed with apocalyptic imagery, building the faith of the Israelites living in exile under Babylonian rule. Daniel remains faithful to the God of Israel, and God allows him to have influence in the surrounding culture of Babylon. His visions offer guidance for faithfulness and hope of a future where evil hearts and rulers will one day come under the authority of the one true God. Daniel's visions also introduce us to the "Son of Man," a Messiah figure who will come to save and restore Israel to their God and bring about a new Jerusalem. Throughout the Gospels (Matthew, Mark, Luke and John), Jesus uses this title, "the Son of Man" to refer to himself. This points back to the prophetic moments in the Hebrew Scriptures and signals his identity <u>as</u> the long-awaited Jewish Messiah. The book of Daniel offers a glimpse of God's plan to restore his people and remain faithful to them no matter how hopeless their circumstances seem.

<u>Encouragement As You Read:</u> Take your time, and take note of anything that stands out as interesting, important or confusing. Write down any questions you have.

<u>SCRIPTURE REFLECTION:</u>

- What stuck out most to you? Why?

- What did you learn about God?

- What did you learn about resistance and trust in God?

- How might God be inviting you to respond?

Saturday | Breakouts:

Breakout 1 | Scripture (Trevor): Knowing and trusting God amidst confusion, doubt and pride. *Can I actually trust the Bible? Why is the Bible so difficult to read? What should I expect from Scripture? How do I spend time in Scripture more consistently?* Join us as we explore these questions and more.

Breakout 2 | Silence & Solitude (Sofia): Experiencing peace and rest amidst busyness and distraction. *Why don't I hear from God?* It's nearly impossible to hear God's voice and be in tune with His direction for our lives if we don't make space to be *with* Him in silence. We live in a culture where busyness, distraction, and constant noise (podcasts, music, tv) is the norm. The result? We are always exhausted and never present. How do we break out of this pattern?

Breakout 3 | Worship (Michael): Practicing Christ-centered worship in a self-centered world. So much of our life is oriented towards fulfilling <u>our</u> desires, accomplishing <u>our</u> goals, and making sure <u>our</u> reputation is well-maintained. What if we were created to live in a totally different way than this? How does putting Jesus at the center create *freedom*? How can we live a life that brings glory to God above all else?

Breakout 4 | Prayer (Natalie): Prayerfulness in an anxious world. *If God is real, why doesn't He take away my anxiety?* Prayer is communion and communication with God where we offer ourselves to Him as we are and receive Him as He is. How do we become prayerful people who resist the tyranny of anxiety and surrender our need to control outcomes?

Saturday | Breakout #1 _____

_____

_____

_____

_____

_____

_____

_____

_____

_____

_____

_____

_____

_____

_____

_____

_____

_____

_____

_____

_____

Saturday | Breakout #2 _____

_____

_____

_____

_____

_____

_____

_____

_____

_____

_____

_____

_____

_____

_____

_____

_____

_____

_____

_____

_____

_____

_____

Saturday | Teaching Notes

Saturday | Church Time

Practices
What was "life-giving"
for you today? Why?
What was challenging?
Why?

_____

_____

_____

_____

_____

_____

_____

_____

_____

_____

_____

_____

People
Who is someone who
included you today? Who is
someone you want to
include better tomorrow?

_____

_____

_____

_____

_____

_____

_____

Main Take Away
What is one thing you heard today that inspired you, convicted you or encouraged you?

I Feel...
What is one feeling word to describe where you at right now?
see p. 58 for a list!

_____
_____
_____
_____
_____
_____
_____
_____
_____
_____
_____
_____
_____
_____
_____
_____
_____

RV Time | Discussion

We are to approach Scripture with humility and wonder as we allow God to use the truth of His Word to transform us in holiness and love. There is endless truth to be discovered in Scripture!

Before discussing, pray as a group and invite the Holy Spirit to teach you. Read the passage all the way through and then, as a group, come up with a question to frame the discussion. What do you want to discover? Seek after truth using the text as a guide and go wherever it leads you!

TOPIC

Submission to God

FOCUS SCRIPTURE

James 4

DISCUSS

What must we resist in order to submit to God?

QUESTIONS

- Why is it difficult to resist?
- What does it mean to submit? Why does God ask us to submit to Him?
- What keeps us from trusting God?
- How might God be inviting you to respond?

SUNDAY

THE TREK

Sunday | Time with God

PRAYER:

Praying Scripture (p.49)

SCRIPTURE:

Psalm 24

Psalm 24 Commentary:

Author: Psalm 24 was written by King David, around 1,000 years before Jesus was born. David reigned over Israel and was beloved by the nation, but he wasn't always wise or even close to morally perfect. David grew up as a humble shepherd and would spend days in solitude, where he developed a very close relationship with God. Later as king, David faced intimidating decisions, intense temptation, and was often on the run from people who wanted him dead. In every season, he turned to the Lord in prayer and wrestled with his feelings, desires, temptations, sin, doubt, limitations and longings for God. This is what most of the Psalms are: real prayers, poems and songs that we can adopt as our own prayers to God.

Overall Theme: God is worthy of our trust and worship. This Psalm highlights God's power, authority and sovereignty over all things.

Encouragement As You Read: Read slowly, taking note of anything that stands out as interesting, important or confusing. Write down any questions you have.

SCRIPTURE REFLECTION:

- What stuck out most? Why?

- Is there a particular truth or insight that is challenging or convicting?

- Is there a particular truth or insight that is encouraging to you?

- How might God be inviting you to respond?

Sunday | Teaching Notes

Sunday | Church Time

Practices
What practice, activity, or rhythm from this trip do you want to integrate into your daily life?

_____
_____
_____
_____
_____
_____
_____
_____
_____
_____
_____
_____
_____
_____

People
Who were you encouraged by today and why? What about them encouraged you?

_____
_____
_____
_____
_____
_____
_____

Main Take Away

What is one truth you discovered today that challenged you?

I Feel...

What is your feeling word for the day?
see p. 58 for a list!

RV Time | Discussion

We are to approach Scripture with humility and wonder as we allow God to use the truth of His Word to transform us in holiness and love. There is endless truth to be discovered in Scripture!

Before discussing, pray as a group and invite the Holy Spirit to teach you. Read the passage all the way through and then, as a group, come up with a question to frame the discussion. What do you want to discover? Seek after truth using the text as a guide and go wherever it leads you!

TOPIC

Resistance & Love

FOCUS SCRIPTURE

Romans 12

DISCUSS

What must we resist in order to love?

QUESTIONS

- What *is* love according to this passage?
- How does "viewing" God's mercy empower you to resist the world?
- How does "not conforming to the patterns of this world" relate to love?
- How would your life be different if you lived in accordance with this passage? Where do you fall short? Where are you compelled or convicted to change?

2 Minute Story

What's Your Story?

When you get home from camp what's the first question your parents, siblings, friends, coach, or neighbor asks? If your people are anything like my people they will ask you, "Hey, how was the Trek? Can you tell me about it?"

Often this question is overwhelming, as it can be hard to articulate an experience on the spot in a way that another person (who wasn't there) can understand. We can use 2-Minute Stories as a meaningful way to share what God did during the Trek.

Use the brainstorming sheet, outline template, and rough drafts, to guide you through your 2-Minute Story creation process. Have fun and make it your own.

Stories are powerful. We have an opportunity to share stories from our weekend that will encourage others and honor God.

RV Time | 2 Minute Story

Here are a few basic instructions to follow that will help you bring shape, structure and direction to your story.

1. **Use an opening sentence (hook) that will capture your reader.**

2. **Use a passage from scripture to support your main takeaway.**

3. **Think of a story that can answer ONE of the following.**

    - What did God teach you about RESISTANCE on this trip?
    - What did you learn about yourself? How did you learn that?
    - What did you learn about God? How did you learn that?
    - How will your life be different because of this trip?

4. **Use some of the following tips when writing your story.**

    - Provide details – specific places, names, titles, etc
    - Use descriptive words – colors, smells, sounds, etc.
        - Be personable – focus on <u>your</u> experience
    - Use 1-2 sentences at the start to describe the trip
    - Have fun with it! it's not for a grade. Enjoy! ☺

RV Time | 2 Minute Story

Use this outline to help organize your ideas, opening and closing sentences. Give yourself a loose roadmap before you start writing.

I. **Title**

_____

II. **Opening Sentence (Hook)**

_____
_____
_____
_____

III. **Body Paragraphs**

    a. What question are you answering?

       _____
       _____

    b. What scripture reference are you sharing?

       _____
       _____

IV. **Closing Sentence (Tie in Your Opening & Conclude Story)**

_____
_____
_____
_____

Now go find a leader to read your outline to. Once they've given input, go write your story!

My Story

Title: _____

Full Name: _____

_____
_____
_____
_____
_____
_____
_____
_____
_____
_____
_____
_____
_____
_____
_____
_____
_____
_____

My Story

My Story

_____

_____

_____

_____

_____

_____

_____

_____

_____

_____

_____

_____

_____

_____

_____

_____

_____

_____

_____

My Story

My Story

My Story

Appendix

Ways To Pray

There are endless ways to pray. Here are some biblical options to help you to practice this foundational rhythm of communion and communication with God:

I. <u>P-R-A-Y</u>

P-ause: Stop, breathe, focus your heart and mind on God.

R-ejoice: Praise God for who He is, what he's done, and offer gratitude for anything that comes to mind.

A-sk: Present any request, desire, need to God. He knows what you ultimately need and loves to bless you.

Y-ield (Yes): Submit to God and where he may be wanting to guide, convict, transform, or renew you (Romans 12:1-2)

II. <u>PRAYING SCRIPTURE</u>

There are hundreds of prayers recorded in scripture. We not only can read and learn from these prayers but we can pray them as our own honest prayers. Here are few references to get you started:
- o **Matthew 6:9-13** (The Lord's Prayer)
- o **Ephesians 1:3-11** (Prayer of Gratitude and Intercession)
- o **Psalm 23** (Prayer for Guidance and Trust)
- o **Psalm 6** (Prayer of Grief)
- o **Psalm 103** (Prayer of Hunger for God)
- o Any and every **Psalm**!

III. <u>THE LORD'S PRAYER</u>

Slowly pray through Jesus' framework for prayer. Contemplate each line as you pray it as your own honest prayer. Follow Matthew 6:9-13:

Our Father...
In Heaven...
Hallowed be Your Name...
Your kingdom come...
Your will be done...
On earth as it is in heaven...
Give us today our daily bread...
And forgive us our debts...
As we also forgive...
And lead us not into temptation...
But deliver us from the evil one

IV. <u>PRAYER OF REPENTANCE</u>

God, You are...
> Describe attributes of God that are in contrast to the sin you are repenting.

I am...
> Describe the state of being that led to your specific sin. What does it feel like? What are you thinking?

I sinned when...
> Describe your sin. What did you do or not do? Why was it sin?

Forgive me...
> Ask God for forgiveness. Acknowledging that you are already forgiven in Jesus.

Make me...

Describe a state of being that you long for but do not currently have.

So that...

Describe the freedom that God's forgiveness will bring and what you will do with it.

Because you are...

Thank God for who He is.

V. <u>PRAYER OF GRATITUDE</u>

I was...

Describe what it was like before God helped you or you knew Him. What were you like before? How did it feel? What were you thinking and feeling?

Then you...

Describe what God did to help you? What was it like? What did it feel like? What were you thinking?

Because you are...

What does your experience reveal about who God is? What attributes did it reveal? What would it look like to worship Him in light of that?

VI. <u>PRAYER OF GRIEF</u>

I am...

Describe your grief. What does it feel like? What thoughts accompany your grief?

Because...

Describe the causes of your grief. What happened?

Yet you are...
> Affirm the aspects of God's character or His promises that are hardest for you to believe (in the context of your current grief).

VIII. <u>INTERCESSORY PRAYER</u>

To intercede means to pray with and/or for someone on their behalf. We can bring others to God and intercede for them just as the Holy Spirit intercedes for us. We have authority in Christ to bring ourselves and others before the throne of God in prayer (Hebrews 4:15-16). There isn't one "right way" to pray for someone but you can start by:

1. Offering him/her by name to God (ex. *"God, I offer my friend Trevor to you on her behalf"*)
2. Thank God for them (*"Thank you for Trevor..."* something you see in them or you sense God sees in them)
3. Ask God for whatever you sense they need based on something they've shared, what you may know about them, or on what the Holy Spirit brings to mind.

VII. <u>BREATH PRAYER</u>

1. Take 3 deep breaths. Breathe 4 seconds in, hold for 7 seconds, and slowly exhale for 8 seconds. Focus only on your breathing.

Now take 3 more breathes imagining that with each breathe you are releasing something to God and receiving Him in some specific way:

2. Breathe out what you need to release <u>to</u> God (anxiety, fear, shame, a dream, a relationship, etc). Be specific.
3. Breathe in and receive what you desire <u>from</u> God (peace, patience, self-control, grace, guidance, etc). Be specific.

How to Read Scripture

The bible or scripture is a library of 66 different books written by 44+ authors over the span of 2,000 years. This, as a whole, communicates one unified and true story that points to Jesus. This story continues with us! Scripture is the ultimate authority on all things true and provides a lens through which we are to view God, ourselves, and the world as it truly is. Every truth and insight is a gift from God to us. As we study and contemplate Scripture, we need to first understand what the author is saying (and ultimately, what God is saying through them). Then, we can focus our heart and mind on that truth and allow God to His transforming work in our heart, mind and soul. As Eugene Peterson said, we must seek to allow scripture to "penetrate the tissues of our lives". Here is simple time tested way to read scripture on its own terms with God's help:

1. **Pray** | "God, focus my heart and mind..."

2. **Context |** When, where, why and to whom was it written?

3. **Read** | Highlight or underline what stands out

4. **Summarize** | What is the overall meaning of the passage? What's being communicated by the author and by God?

5. **Ask** | What questions do you have? Write them down to revisit with a study Bible, trusted mentor or Bible commentary?

6. **Discover** | What insight(s) or truth(s) did you discover?

7. **Respond |** Pray, "God how do you want me to respond to this?"

Silence and Solitude

We live in a cultural moment of over-commitment, busyness, and constant distraction. It's nearly impossible to align our hearts and minds with God and His transformative work if we don't make space and time to be *with* Him alone in the quiet. Silence & Solitude is a simple way for us as followers of Jesus to do just that. It's a moment of intentional time spent alone with God in silence. This is the foundation in which all other spiritual practices can be built upon.

Jesus "often got away to lonely places to pray" (Luke 5:16) in the midst of constant responsibilities and needs around him. In this rhythm of *solitude* Jesus connected with the Father, rested in Him, and received guidance and direction. This is a core practice for us to engage in as we follow Jesus. Silence and Solitude helps us submit to God's authority, receive His grace, and follow His guidance. There could not be a more important time for us to immerse ourselves in this. Dallas Willard says:

"Solitude well practiced will break the power of busyness, hurry, isolation, and loneliness. You will see that the world is not on your shoulders after all. You will find yourself, and God will find you in new ways. Silence also brings Sabbath [to stop; to cease; rest] to you. It completes solitude, for without it you cannot be alone. Far from being a mere absence, silence allows the reality of God to stand in the midst of your life. God does not ordinarily compete for our attention. In silence we come to attend."

— *Dallas Willard, The Great Omission: Reclaiming Jesus's Essential Teachings on Discipleship*

John Mark Comer clarifies: *"To be clear, the goal here is simply to 'be with Jesus.' Don't feel like you have to "do" anything. Just relax and enjoy his presence. In silence we sit in the quiet reality of the moment, allowing our anxiety, hopes, fears and thoughts come to the surface with God. This makes the solitude part so important, solitude is not isolation, it's getting away to a quiet place to be with God, 'as Jesus often did'."*

This practice is not the same as New Age practices like "mindfulness" or meditation. Those have the goal of finding the answers in the self and achieving "inner peace". In the way of Jesus, silence and solitude is a rhythm of consistently turning our attention to God in the quiet place. Sometimes we may experience peace and calm from spending time with God, but more often, in moments of silence we are confronted with what's really going on within us: anxiety, unsettled thoughts, lingering shame, imaginary future hard conversations, deep-seeded bitterness, sadness, hopes and dreams. These can flood our minds as soon as we tune out distractions and noise. Silence is also where we can be confronted with the enemies of God: the world, the flesh and the Devil, which are working against us to deter us from living in alignment with God. This is why it is so important to root ourselves in the truth of Scripture often, especially *before* we enter silence & solitude.

At times, silence can be difficult and particularly for some of us who already have difficulty focusing for periods of time. But you are capable! If you can take the risk of and allow silence and solitude to become a normal rhythm, you may find that the "noise" of life settles and you're able to receive and experience God's grace more clearly and often.

Silence & Solitude | How?

Put away any distractions, settle into a comfortable setting, and feel free to move, walk, stretch and go to different places throughout your time. The following steps are not a "have to" but a framework from common spiritual practices. There is freedom and flexibility in this!

- Anchor in Scripture: Start by reading a Psalm or any familiar scripture passage a few times slowly to anchor your heart and mind in the reality of God with you. Some possible anchor scriptures:
    - Psalm 23
    - Psalm 24
    - Psalm 103
    - Psalm 139
    - John 15:1-8
    - Philippians 4:4-8
- Breath Prayer:
    - Close your eyes
    - Breath in count to 4, hold for 6, breath out count to 5
    - Just focus on breathing, let your thoughts go
    - Don't worry if your mind wanders
    - When you notice your mind start to wander, just recenter with a quick prayer, like, "Lord Jesus have mercy on me..." or "Holy Spirit come..." and come back to your breathing.
- Relax: Let your soul "catch up to your body". Acknowledge how you are feeling. Continue breathing and physically relax. There's nowhere else you need to be right now.

- <u>Abide</u>: Acknowledge God with you and you with Him. You are united with Christ, by the love of the Father and the power of the Holy Spirit. He is within you, lovingly guiding you towards deeper union and maturity. Rest in his love for you and receive whatever He wants to give you.
- **Pray:** Close in a prayer of gratitude, confession or request and commit the rest of your day to God.

Keep these in mind:

- You can't "succeed" or "fail" at this practice. All you can do is show up. Remember to be patient with God and yourself. This takes some people years to master. Resist the urge to say, "I'm bad at this" or "This isn't for me", or judge yourself.
- If sitting still is hard for you, you might want to try this while going on a walk somewhere quiet and distraction-free.
    - Apply the same idea to a walking prayer and focus on your walking instead of your breathing.
- Remember:
    - Boredom isn't bad, can lead to discovery
    - Let your mind wander, invite God into it
    - Ask, "God, what do you have for me in this?"
    - Use a journal or the pages below to write thoughts, insights, truths, etc.
    - Put your phone away, use a watch if you need to keep track of the time

Feeling Word List

Identifying and communicating how we feel is an important part of understanding how to love and receive love from both God and others. It is often difficult for us to articulate what we are feeling. Here is a non-extensive list to help:

HAPPY, cheerful, delighted, elated, encouraged, glad, gratified, joyful, lighthearted, overjoyed, pleased, relieved, satisfied, thrilled, secure, optimistic

LOVING, affectionate, cozy, passionate, warm, tender, responsive, thankful, appreciative, refreshed, pleased, comforted, reassured

HIGH ENERGY, energetic, enthusiastic, excited, playful, rejuvenated, talkative, pumped, motivated, driven, determined, obsessed, jittery, giggly

AMAZED, stunned, surprised, shocked, jolted, enlightened

ANXIOUS, afraid, uneasy, nauseated, nervous, restless, preoccupied, worried, scared, tense, fearful, terrified, insecure, indecisive, hyper-vigilant, cautious

CONFIDENT, positive, secure, self-assured, assertive

PEACEFUL, relieved, at ease, calm, comforted, cool, relaxed, composed, protected

OVERWHELMED, apprehensive, boxed in, burdened, confused, distressed, guarded, hard-pressed, paralyzed, panicky, tense, weighted down, edgy

TRAUMATIZED, shocked, disturbed, injured, damaged, unloved, unlovable, hated

ANGRY, annoyed, controlled, manipulated, furious, grouchy, grumpy, irritated, provoked, frustrated, hateful, cold, icy, bitter cynical

LOW ENERGY, beaten down, exhausted, tired, weak, listless, depressed, detached, withdrawn, indifferent, apathetic, lazy, bored

ALONE, avoidant, lonely, abandoned, deserted, isolated, cut off, detached, disconnected, unwanted

SAD, unhappy, crushed, dejected, depressed, desperate, hopeless, grieved, heavy, despairing, weepy

BETRAYED, deceived, fooled, duped, tricked, misled, skeptical

CONFUSED, baffled, perplexed, mystified, bewildered, misunderstood, disoriented

ASHAMED, guilty, mortified, humiliated, embarrassed, exposed, stupid

DISAPPOINTED, let down, disheartened, disillusioned, distrustful

INVISIBLE, forgotten, overlooked, unimportant, invisible, disregarded, lost

DESPISED, ridiculed, dumb, belittled, mocked, scorned, shamed, hated, detested

Milan and Kay Yerkovich ©2014 howwelove.com | Soul Words

KP Schedule

KP (Kitchen Patrol) is a great way for each of us to pitch in and help get our meals prepped and cleaned up! Everyone from your RV must be present at KP, failure to do so will result in dock time. **KP 1** for breakfast is **15** minutes BEFORE. **KP 1** for lunch/dinner is **30** minutes BEFORE. **KP 2** is immediately AFTER a meal (cleanup).

FRIDAY
Dinner KP 2: **RV #1** (30 min before)

SATURDAY
Breakfast KP 1: **RV #2** (15 min before)
Breakfast KP 2: **RV #3** (immediately after - cleanup)

Lunch KP 1: **RV #4** (30 min before)
Lunch KP 2: **RV #5** (immediately after - cleanup)

Dinner KP 1: **RV #6** (30 min before)
Dinner KP 2: **RV #7** (immediately after - cleanup)

SUNDAY
Breakfast KP 1: **RV #8** (15 min before)
Breakfast KP 2: **RV #9** (immediately after - cleanup)

Lunch KP 1: **RV #1** (30 min before)
Lunch KP 2: **RV #2** (immediately after - cleanup)

Dinner KP 1: **RV #3** (30 min before)
Dinner KP 2: **RV #4** (immediately after - cleanup)

MONDAY
KP 1: **Leaders**

LEADER GUIDE

THE TREK

Leaders,

It is such a blessing to journey alongside youth in their lives and discipleship to Jesus. Thank you for giving up time with family, friends, work and rest to serve OVERFLOW youth in this way.

Our unity as a leadership team is one of the most important ways we can love students this weekend. If we are not on the same page with anything, please refer to this leader guidebook and if there is still not clarity talk with Trevor.

Lastly, it's important that we lead by example in everything from our attitude to how we participate in all aspects of the trip. God has been looking forward to this time with you. Enjoy it with Him!

With Love,

OVERFLOW STAFF

RV Check-In Process

RV CHECK-IN SET UP:
All items you need are found in your RV Box and RV Bag. Mark off each of the items as you complete them:

- Put on wristband on your right wrist
- Driver: complete RV Training & Check-List
- *Read the Grey water, Brown water, and Generator Instructions*

Non Driver Leader:
- Find a good place for your Paper Towels (1 roll)
- Place Toilet Paper in bathroom (3 rolls)
- Find a good place for your Brown Mat, Blue Tarp and Grass mat (used at Refugio)
- Set up Walkie-Talkie Charging Station (2 chargers)
- Plug in Car Charger & Cord
- Grab Bluetooth Speaker
  - o Turn It On
  - o Connect to your Phone
  - o Only play **appropriate** Music (when in doubt – Worship music!)
- Set Up Student Package on table or couch
  - o OVERFLOW Wristband
  - o Sweatshirt
  - o Journal
  - o Pen
  - o Highlighter
- Prop open door for easy access all morning
- Largely & clearly label RV Name on front & back

RV Check-In Process

STUDENT CHECK-IN PROCESS:
Students will show up to you with a Name Tag after being signed in on CCB under the OVERFLOW Tent.

LEADERS:
One leader will first welcome your students to your RV. Your main role is to keep your students in your RV until given further instructions. As a reminder, you are in-charge of the following:

- Cross their name off of your roster.
- Put On OVERFLOW Wristband
- Give them their Student Package
- Ask if they have any medication - if so have them go check it in with OVERFLOW staff
- IceBreaker / Hang out
- Wait and hang out until you get the word over your Walkie-Talkie to depart for the destination

AT NO TIME ARE LEADERS & STUDENTS TO LEAVE RV – USE YOUR WALKIE TALKIE TO COMMUNICATE NEEDS. BATHROOM AS GROUP WHEN PROMPTED

THE TREK 2025

RHYTHMS OF RESISTANCE

Leader Protocol

Remember that you are driving parents' CHILDREN. Safety is our #1 priority while driving these vehicles. Always use the motto, "it's safe to be safe" when driving. Follow these guidelines otherwise you will be asked to no longer drive:

DRIVING GUIDELINES:
- Stick to the Speed Limit
- Stay in Caravan Order
- Use Your Turn Signals Always
- Follow All Traffic Laws
- Pre-Trip Checks of Vehicles Friday & Monday
- Check Tires (inflated, no punctures, etc.)
- Oil is full
- Blinkers
- Headlights
- Walk around vehicle
- Check Gas
- Must get adequate sleep the night before driving
- Must have a passenger at all times (leader or student)
- No pulling over
- No texting, changing the music or talking on the phone while driving

NON-DRIVER PROTOCOL:
You will be required to have a passenger sitting next to you at all times. You can empower different students throughout each drive to play this role or let them rotate each hour. Use this time as intentional space to pour into the life of a student. Communicate this with passenger:
- In charge of music, communication, air conditioning, & directions
- Their job is to keep you engaged & distraction FREE
- This can be your first float together for the weekend.

WALKIE-TALKIE PROTOCOL:

Walkie-Talkies can make our lives as leaders very convenient when needing to communicate with each other in regards to directions, emergencies etc. Please keep these on you at all times and know that these are not meant for fun, but for business.

1. Only Used For "safety and communication" Purposes
2. Students Can't Use (Except Passenger)
3. Keep Charged
4. Keep On You At All Times
5. Don't Lose
6. Use Walkie-Talkie Lingo
7. Speak Clearly

WALKIE-TALKIE LINGO:

When talking on your walkie-talkie try to use this simple lingo to make sure everyone is on the same page. Please start off each conversation addressing whom you are talking to. If you need a private conversation with a leader, ask them to switch to a different channel. End each conversation with a *10-4* so we know you understand. Speak clearly and concisely when talking into your walkie-talkie.

- "[Name 1] to [Name 2]" → ex: *"Trevor to Nat"*
- "Go for [Name 2]" → *ex: "Go for Nat"*
- "10-4" = "Okay, I understand"
- "What's your TBC?" = "What's Your Total Body Count?"

- "Over" = "Finish Conversation"

RV PROTOCOL:

While we are in RV's it is important that we keep these factors in mind in order to keep a safe environment for our students:

1. READ GREY WATER, BROWN WATER, GENERATOR INSTRUCTIONS and inform your RV of the protocol.
2. Appropriate music only and keep at a **low volume** (when in doubt, play worship)
3. Keep the RV clean ("don't put it down, put it away")
4. No jumping ever!
5. Keep conversations appropriate and above reproach
6. Put seatbelts on while driving. No standing or walking around while the RV is moving

Refer back to Guidelines and Expectations

SAFETY / MEDICAL PROTOCOL:

The safety of our students is our number one priority. Please follow these guidelines below when needed:

1. Fill-Out an Incident Report When Needed
2. "Safe To Be Safe"
3. One leader will distribute student medications
4. Only OVERFLOW staff can distribute non-prescribed, (over-the-counter) counter medication

RV TIME:

Spend a couple minutes each morning as co-leads preparing for your RV time. Remember, you're journeying with your students.

MEALS:
Meals are a great time to spend in community. Everyone will be eating together and at the same time. Remember we will always pray before we eat & the ladies will go first. Every RV will serve on KP (some twice) before (KP 1) or after (KP 2) a meal

CO-ED DYNAMICS:
Having guys and girls in RVs together is an intentional way for us to encourage healthy opposite sex relationships in the context of the body of Christ. This is an opportunity for young men to grow in chivalry, love and honor towards young women as their sisters in Christ. And young women would grow in respect and trust for their brothers in Christ. This requires us as leaders to not only model this but to keep students accountable. This starts with setting the intention, clear boundaries and communicating well. Do everything you can to be aware of dynamics and speak into anything if necessary. Guys and girls should never be alone together or sleep next to each other. If there are dynamics that you are concerned about please communicate with OVERFLOW staff to discern the best way to care for the students in your RV. Be mindful, not fearful. Be empowering, not demanding.

FLOATS (ONE-ON-ONES):
Meet with each of your students once this weekend. The goal is for your students to be known. (aim for 30 min)

Leader Agreement

Being a leader is a great responsibility. Beyond what we teach with our words, we know the greatest testimony to our youth is our own lives as we follow Jesus. As a part of the responsibility of being a leader, we ask you to agree to each of the following statements:

Relationship with God: Jesus Christ is my Lord and Savior. I have surrendered my life to Him, and I am committed to following Jesus and His way of life. I commit to cultivating my personal relationship with God by spending time in His word, in prayer, and other means of being with God. I agree to the values of Grace Fellowship Church.

Mindful of My Role: I understand my primary responsibility is to love the students assigned to me in my RV towards Jesus. I understand my role as a counselor and will look to OVERFLOW Staff for guidance and support.

Mindful of How I Live: As a leader, I understand following the way of Jesus and living above reproach is as important as anything.

Personal Health: I recognize that being healthy physically, spiritually and emotionally are priorities in order for me to lead. I commit to making healthy choices as I follow Jesus. I will communicate with OVERFLOW staff for additional support or guidance.

Mindful of What I Wear: I commit to being mindful of what I wear and will avoid wearing things like yoga pants, short shorts, tight athletic shorts, low cut shirts, etc. I will model modesty and personal style. *This applies to both male and female leaders.*

Inappropriate Student Relationships: I will avoid even the appearance of inappropriate relationships with students. For example, I will:

- Only show appropriate affection to students – especially towards those of the opposite sex such that my behavior cannot be questioned.
- Not use any flirtatious or suggestive language, even in jest, which could be misinterpreted or could cause some offense.
- Use discretion in correspondence to members of the opposite sex.
- Avoid one-on-one with a member of the opposite sex.
- Avoid one-on-one appointments with a member of the same sex where such behavior could be questioned.
  - o Never be alone with doors closed
  - o Be mindful of physical boundaries

Defend the Team: I will never slander or speak disrespectfully about any other member of the Leadership Team. If I have an issue with another leader, I will communicate the issue directly with that leader in a spirit of grace and gentleness and/or I will elicit the help of a youth staff leader to facilitate a process of healthy communication with that leader. I will keep the problems and issues of the team within the confines of the team and commit to working them out together.

Confidentiality: If there is anything shared that puts into question the emotional or physical safety of a student, parent, or leader, I will report directly to OVERFLOW staff to discern the best process to support and care for that student. I understand that I do not need to initially disclose the name of that person to the OVERFLOW staff. I will never promise confidentiality, but if confidentiality is requested I will respond with:

"I can't promise confidentiality but I can promise that your safety and care is my #1 priority and I will only share for that reason. And I will tell you before I share with anyone and if there are options I will give you that."

Lastly, anything shared by a student, parent, or leader is always to be handled with wisdom, discernment and compassion.

I hereby acknowledge my understanding and agreement with the statements contained in this agreement and will strive to live according to them. I understand and recognize that failing to acknowledge or follow any of these commitments above could result in conversation with youth staff and potential termination as a leader from the trip.

X: _____   _____

Signature   Date

X: _____

   Print Name

Confiscation List

If you confiscate a cell phone, iPad, or any other prohibited item please list the student's name, the day you took it, what you took, and give the device to Trevor. Make sure they get these back upon arrival at the church. Please give all Amnesty Items to Jessica upon arrival at camp.

STUDENT NAME   **ITEM**

1. _____   _____

2. _____   _____

3. _____   _____

4. _____   _____

5. _____   _____

6. _____   _____

7. _____   _____

8. _____   _____

Incident Report

If an injury happens, please walkie Trevor immediately. Please complete this form anytime you work with a student for health purposes or an injury. Trevor will make parent phone calls with every Incident Report logged, so please be detailed. Medication distribution does not require an Incident Report.

Name of Student _____

Date _____

Time _____

Description of Incident/Injury/Illness

_____

_____

_____

Place of Incident/Injury

_____

_____

Staff Witness

_____

_____

First Aid Administered (Including medications given)

_____

_____

_____

_____

Were parents contacted? Yes____ No_____ Time_____

Was a hospital visit necessary? Yes_____ No_____

Hospital name: _____

Was the child's personal Physician contacted? Yes___No___

Leader Signature: _____

Incident Report

If an injury happens, please walkie Trevor immediately. Please complete this form anytime you work with a student for health purposes or an injury. Trevor will make parent phone calls with every Incident Report logged, so please be detailed. Medication distribution does not require an Incident Report.

Name of Student _____
Date _____
Time _____

Description of Incident/Injury/Illness
_____
_____
_____

Place of Incident/Injury
_____
_____

Staff Witness
_____
_____

First Aid Administered (Including medications given)
_____
_____
_____
_____

Were parents contacted? Yes____ No____ Time_____

Was a hospital visit necessary? Yes_____ No_____

Hospital name:

Was the child's personal Physician contacted? Yes___No___

Leader Signature: _____

Incident Report

If an injury happens, please walkie Trevor immediately. Please complete this form anytime you work with a student for health purposes or an injury. Trevor will make parent phone calls with every Incident Report logged, so please be detailed. Medication distribution does not require an Incident Report.

Name of Student _____

Date _____

Time _____

Description of Incident/Injury/Illness

_____
_____
_____

Place of Incident/Injury

_____
_____

Staff Witness

_____
_____

First Aid Administered (Including medications given)

_____
_____
_____
_____

Were parents contacted? Yes____ No_____ Time_____

Was a hospital visit necessary? Yes_____ No_____

Hospital name: _____

Was the child's personal Physician contacted? Yes___No___

Leader Signature: _____

Incident Report

If an injury happens, please walkie Trevor immediately. Please complete this form anytime you work with a student for health purposes or an injury. Trevor will make parent phone calls with every Incident Report logged, so please be detailed. Medication distribution does not require an Incident Report.

Name of Student _____
Date _____
Time _____

Description of Incident/Injury/Illness
_____
_____
_____

Place of Incident/Injury
_____
_____

Staff Witness
_____
_____

First Aid Administered (Including medications given)
_____
_____
_____
_____

Were parents contacted? Yes___ No____ Time_____

Was a hospital visit necessary? Yes_____ No_____

Hospital name: _____

Was the child's personal Physician contacted? Yes___No___

Leader Signature: _____

Directions to Refugio

From Grace Fellowship Church:

- Turn Left onto Red Hill AVe
- Turn Right onto Bristol
- Continue onto Bristol
- Use the right lane to turn right onto I-405 N
- Keep left at the fork to stay on I-405 N (for 39.9mi)
- Use the right 3 lanes to merge onto US-101 N toward Ventura (for 101mi)
- Take exit 120 for Refugio Rd

10. Turn Left
11. Arrive at **35 Refugio Rd, Goleta, CA 93117**

SCHEDULE

THE TREK

Thursday, January 16, 2025

11:45a | Lunch at Grace
12:00p | Leave for El Monte
1:00p | Pick Up Units | El Monte
- o Driver Training
- o Head back and forth until we have all 10 units
- o Have someone at church getting check-in set up

03:00 | Check In Ready | GFC Parking Lot
04:00 | Check In | GFC Parking Lot
- • All Student and Leader luggage drop off
- • RV boxes into RVs

06:15p | Clean & Lock Up | GFC Parking Lot

Friday, January 17th

08:00a | Leader Orientation | GFC
  o   Eat food & coffee
08:30a | Finalize Rv Set Up | GFC
  o   Non-driver setup RVs with RV boxes
10:00a | Student Check-In | GFC
  o   Refer to **pg. 63-66**
10:30a | Student Orientation | HS Room
  o   Refer to **pg. 65**
11:30a | Depart | Refugio, CA
12:30p | Lunch: <u>Packed Lunches</u>
  o   Pray as OVERFLOW Family & eat together
03:30p | Arrival | Refugio State Beach
  o   Hang Time in RVs until parked
  o   Drivers work with Trevor for RV formation set-up
04:00p | Camp Set Up | Wait in RVs until Instructed
  o   Set up RVs
05:00p | Church Time | Main Pit
  o   Prayer, Housekeeping, Worship
  o   Debrief section of journals
06:00p | Dinner: Chicken tenders, grilled chicken, mac &
cheese, mini corn dogs, fries & caesar salad
          KP2: RV #1
07:45p | RV Time #1 | In RVs
  o   "Where are you at with God?" Picture Exercise
08:45p | Set up sleeping areas (beds, sleeping bags)
9:00p | S'mores
10:00p | Lights Out | RVs
  o   Students in RV & Sleeping Bags
  o   Respect Refugio quiet hours
  o   Leaders in charge of quieting your RV
10:15p | Leader Debrief | Kitchen Pit

CATERING: (805) 680-7250
FIREWOOD: (805)795-7111

Saturday, January 18th

07:30a | Coffee & Leader Meeting (15 min)
08:00a | Student Wake Up
08:15a | Breakfast: <u>Grab & Go style</u> (cereal, yogurt, etc.)
    KP1: RV #2 @ 8:00a
    KP2: RV #3 @8:30a
    o We'll Pray ALL Together, Then Eat
08:45a | Morning Meeting| Fire Pit Area
09:00a | Time With God | Around Camp
    o Trevor will brief by campfire before sending off
    o Students to keep within distance of others
    o No talking
    o Bring bible, journal, & pen
10:00a | Morning Time Debrief | Main Pit
10:15a | Breakouts (pick 2 out of 4)
    o Breakout 1@ main pit
    o Breakout 2 @ kitchen pit
    o Breakout 3 @ beach
    o Breakout 4 @ lower picnic tables
11:15a | #off @ Main Pit and Prayer
11:30a | Lunch: <u>Sandwiches</u>
    KP1: RV #4 @11:45a
    KP2: RV #5 @ 12:15p
12:15p | Free Time | Around Camp
    o Worship Rehearsal (11:00am-11:20am)
    o Hike
    o Craft
    o Board Rentals – Sign up @ Info Center
    o Floats
1:00p | Surf or Football Comp | Meet at main Pit
04:00p | Camp Transition| Around Camp
    o Students get ready for dinner
04:45p | Prayer & Debrief | Main Pit
05:30p | Dinner: Tacos (asada, chicken, chorizo, rice, beans)
    KP1: RV #6 @ 5:15p
    KP2: RV #7 @ 6:15p

- o   We'll pray as a group & then eat

07:00p | Church Time| Main Pit
- o   Prayer, Teaching, Worship & Affirmations
- o   Housekeeping if needed
- o   ALL around campfire
- o   Bring journals & dress warm
- o   Hot Cocoa & Coffee available

08:00p | Discussion | In RVs
- o   Guide in Journals

9:15p | Smores | Both Pits

10:15p | RV Quiet Hours| RVs
- o   Students in RV
- o   Respect park quiet hours
- o   Leaders in charge of quieting your RV

10:30p | Leader Debrief | Kitchen Pit

Sunday, January 19th

07:30a | Coffee & Leader Meeting (15 min)
08:00a | Student Wake Up
08:15a | Breakfast: <u>Pancakes</u>
    KP1: RV #8 @ 8:00a
    KP2: RV #9 @ 8:30a
  o We'll Pray ALL Together, Then Eat
08:45a | Morning Meeting | Main Pit
09:00a | Time With God | Around Camp
  o Trevor will brief by campfire before sending off
  o Students to keep within distance of others
  o No talking
  o Bring bible, journal, & pen
09:45a |Morning Time Debrief | Main Pit
10:00a | Guy / Girl Time
10:30a |RV Clean Up | OVERFLOW Staff will judge
11:15a | Free Time| Around Camp
  o Worship Rehearsal (11:15am-11:30am)
  o Craft
  o Board Rentals – Sign up @ Info Center
  o Floats
11:45a | #off and prayer @ Main Pit
12:00p | Lunch: <u>Sandwiches</u>
    KP1: RV #10 @ 11:45a
    KP2: RV #1 @ 12:15p
12:30p | Free Time | Around Camp
  o Craft
  o Beach
  o Board Rentals – Sign up @ Info Center
  o Floats
01:00p | Football or Surf Comp | Meet at main Pit
03:45p | Camp Transition | Around Camp
  o Students get ready for dinner
04:30p | Prayer & Debrief | Main Pit
05:30p | Dinner: Hamburger & Hot Dogs
    KP1: RV #2 @ 5:15p

KP2: RV #3 @ 6:15p
- o   We'll pray as a group & then eat

07:00p | Church Time| Main Pit
- o   Prayer, Teaching, Worship & Affirmations
- o   Housekeeping if needed
- o   ALL around campfire
- o   Bring journals & dress warm
- o   Hot Cocoa & Coffee available

08:00p | RV Time | Discussion

09:15p | Smores | Main Pit

10:15p | RV Quiet Hours | RVs
- o   Students in RV & sleeping bags
- o   Respect park quiet hours
- o   Leaders in charge of quieting your RV

10:30p | Leader Debrief | Kitchen Pit

Monday, January 20th

06:30a | Leader Prayer | Kitchen Fire Pit
07:00a | Breakfast: <u>Grab & Go</u>
     KP1: LEADERS @ 6:45a
- Pray ALL together
- Grab food and head to morning devo

07:30a | Morning Meeting | Main Pit
- Give Instruction for the Morning

08:00a | Two Minute Stories | In RVs
- Guide in journals
- During this time leaders split up ALL food between the RVs

09:00a | Clean Up | All Camp
- 1 trash bag/RV
- Clean RVs
- Pick up trash
- Return picnic tables

10:00a | Depart for GFC
- <u>Lunch will be as we're driving home</u>
- 76 Gas (20 Winchester Canyon Road)
- Chick-Fil-A (3707 State Street) - pick up and meet at Gas

01:30p | Arrival | GFC
1. 1 trash bag/RV
2. Clean RVs
3. Pick up trash

02:15p | Depart for El Monte
- <u>All drivers must drive their unit back to El Monte</u>

03:00p | Drop Off | El Monte

FLOATS

THE TREK

Float Introduction

This weekend you have the unique opportunity to create memories and invest in the lives of the students in your RV.

Conversations with someone a little farther along in the journey is one the coolest ways God often works. Meet with each student in your group (same gender) this weekend at least once for a minimum of 30 minutes to check in with them, get to know them, listen, and conclude your time by praying with them.

Remember: you don't have the power to solve all their problems or the ability to answer all their questions, but you can faithfully point them to Jesus.

Here are some simple questions to help you to start this dialogue.

QUESTIONS:
- How are you doing this weekend?
- What is something you want me to know about you?
- What are you enjoying in life right now?
- What is something difficult or challenging in your life?
- Is there anything you sense God is stirring in you?

Follow up on anything they have shared during RV time, meals, etc.

Float Schedule

Use this to keep track of your floats with students:

1. _____ @ _____

2. _____ @ _____

3. _____ @ _____

4. _____ @ _____

5. _____ @ _____

Debrief Outline | Friday

Number Off & Dock Time

_____

_____

_____

_____

ii. Expectations / Housekeeping / Calendar Reminders

    a. Don't use the kitchen (or take food) unless asked to help
    b. RV Bathroom use reminders (keep it clean)
    c. Drink Water (where to find it)
    d. Surfboards (store _____)
    e. Wet Clothes (hang them _____)
    f. No shoes inside the RV

_____

_____

_____

_____

_____

_____

_____

_____

_____

_____

_____

_____

_____

_____

_____

_____

_____

iii. Group Affirmations

_____
_____
_____
_____

iv. Leader Affirmations

- _____
- _____
- _____

v. Final Reminders

_____
_____
_____
_____
_____
_____

vi. Student's Journal Time & Debrief

_____
_____
_____

vii. Feeling Words

_____
_____
_____

viii. Dismiss back to RV | Prayer Walk

_____
_____
_____

Debrief Outline | Saturday

Number Off & Dock Time

_____
_____
_____
_____

ii. Expectations / Housekeeping / Calendar Reminders

_____
_____
_____
_____
_____
_____
_____
_____
_____
_____
_____
_____
_____
_____
_____
_____
_____
_____
_____
_____
_____
_____

iii. Group Affirmations

_____
_____
_____
_____

iv. Leader Affirmations

- _____
- _____
- _____

v. Final Reminders

_____
_____
_____
_____
_____

vi. Student's Journal Time & Debrief

_____
_____
_____

vii. Feeling Words

_____
_____
_____

viii. Dismiss back to RV | Prayer Walk

_____
_____
_____

Debrief Outline | Sunday

Number Off & Dock Time

_____
_____
_____
_____

ii. Expectations / Housekeeping / Calendar Reminders

_____
_____
_____
_____
_____
_____
_____
_____
_____
_____
_____
_____
_____
_____
_____
_____
_____
_____
_____
_____
_____
_____
_____
_____

iii. Group Affirmations

_____
_____
_____
_____

iv. Leader Affirmations

- _____
- _____
- _____

v. Final Reminders

_____
_____
_____
_____
_____
_____

vi. Student's Journal Time & Debrief

_____
_____
_____

vii. Feeling Words

_____
_____
_____

viii. Dismiss back to Cabins | Prayer Walk

_____
_____
_____

- Dismiss back to RVs in Prayer Walk

NOTES

THE TREK

Notes

Notes

Notes

Notes

Notes

Notes

Notes

Notes

Notes

Notes

Notes

Notes

Notes

Notes

Notes

Notes

Notes

Notes

Notes

Notes

Notes

Notes

Notes

Notes

WORSHIP

THE TREK

ALL HAIL KING JESUS

VERSE 1
There was a moment when the lights went out
When death had claimed its victory
The King of Love had given up His life
The darkest day in history
There on a cross they made for sinners
For every curse His blood atoned
One final breath and it was finished
But not the end we could have known

PRE CHORUS
For the earth began to shake
And the veil was torn
What sacrifice was made
As the heavens roared

CHORUS
All hail King Jesus
All hail the Lord of Heaven and earth
All hail King Jesus
All hail the Savior of the world

VERSE 2
There was a moment when the sky lit up
A flash of light breaking through
When all was lost He crossed eternity
The King of life was on the move
For in a dark, cold tomb
Where our Lord was laid
One miraculous breath
And we're forever changed

CHORUS

BRIDGE
Let every knee, come bow before the King of Kings
Let every tongue, confess that He is Lord
Lift up your shout, let us join with all of Heaven
Singing Holy, Singing Holy
We cry out Holy, we're singing Holy

CHORUS

I SURRENDER ALL

VERSE 1
All to Jesus I surrender
All to Him I freely give
I will ever love and trust Him
In His presence daily live

CHORUS
I surrender all
I surrender all
All to Thee my blessed Savior
I surrender all

VERSE 2
All to Jesus I surrender
All to Him I freely give
I will ever love and trust Him
In His presence daily live

CHORUS

VERSE 3
All to Jesus I surrender
Lord, I give myself to Thee;
Fill me with Thy love and power,
Let Thy blessing fall on me

CHORUS

WE FALL DOWN / WORTHY OF IT ALL

VERSE
We fall down, we lay our crowns
At the feet of Jesus
The greatness of mercy and love
At the feet of Jesus

PRE CHORUS
we cry holy, holy, holy
we cry holy, holy, holy
we cry holy, holy, holy
Is the Lamb

CHORUS
You are worthy of it all, you are worthy of it all
For from you are all things, and to you are all things
You deserve the glory

VERSE

PRE CHORUS

CHORUS

BRIDGE
All the saints and angels bow before your throne
All the elders cast their crowns before the Lamb of God and
sing

CHORUS

YET NOT I BUT THROUGH CHRIST IN ME

VERSE 1
What gift of grace is Jesus my redeemer
There is no more for heaven now to give
He is my joy, my righteousness, and freedom
My steadfast love, my deep and boundless peace

CHORUS 1
To this I hold, my hope is only Jesus
For my life is wholly bound to His
Oh how strange and divine, I can sing, "All is mine"
Yet not I, but through Christ in me

VERSE 2
The night is dark but I am not forsaken
For by my side, the Saviour He will stay
I labor on in weakness and rejoicing
For in my need, His power is displayed

CHORUS 2
To this I hold, my Shepherd will defend me
Through the deepest valley He will lead
Oh the night has been won, and I shall overcome
Yet not I, but through Christ in me

VERSE 3
No fate I dread, I know I am forgiven
The future sure, the price it has been paid
For Jesus bled and suffered for my pardon
And He was raised to overthrow the grave

CHORUS 3
To this I hold, my sin has been defeated
Jesus now and ever is my plea
Oh the chains are released, I can sing, "I am free"
Yet not I, but through Christ in me

VERSE 4
With every breath I long to follow Jesus
For He has said that He will bring me home
And day by day I know He will renew me
Until I stand with joy before the throne

CHORUS 4
To this I hold, my hope is only Jesus
All the glory evermore to Him
When the race is complete, still my lips shall repeat
Yet not I, but through Christ in me

Made in the USA
Las Vegas, NV
10 December 2024

13804092R00075